THE NEED MEETER™

All scripture references, unless otherwise indicated, are taken from the King James Version (KJV) of the Holy Bible.

Other versions:
New International Version (NIV) Amplified Version (AMP)

The Need Meeter™
Is a trademark of Dr. Robert Mukes

God's Ways of Meeting Your Financial Need$™
Is a trademark of Dr. Robert Mukes

Wisdom of Wealth™
Is a trademark of Dr. Robert Mukes

First Printing 2005
Library of Congress Control Number: 2010908022
ISBN 978-0-9701799-5-1

Second Printing 2025
ISBN 978-0-9701799-1-3

Published in Southaven, Mississippi, by Faith Food, LLC. Printed in the United States of America, and distributed by Faith Food, LLC, Southaven, Mississippi.

Cover and logos design by Robert Mukes

Dedication

This book is dedicated to my late parents
Robert and Mentie Mukes,
who have entered into their eternal rest.

LEARN: GOD'S WAYS OF MEETING YOUR FINANCIAL NEED$™

~Jehovah Jireh~

FAITH FOOD™
THE LIVING BREAD

THE NEED MEETER™

By

Dr. Robert Mukes

CONTENTS

INTRODUCTION

The world has reached a time in eternity in which man is faced with acknowledging who his real source truly is. Man's belief system is being challenged as never before. You can clearly see that the whole world is beginning to experience a tremendous financial crisis. God is honoring His transfer of wealth covenant (Psalms 111:5-6). This is God releasing the wealth of the world kingdoms and disobedient saints and transferring it to the eternal Kingdom of God (Ecclesiastes 2:26; Proverbs 28:8; Matthew 25:14-30; Revelation 11:15). God is anointing the ministers of finance (treasurers - Nehemiah 13:13; Acts 7:10), as His instruments to facilitate this kingdom transfer. Why ? to establish His everlasting covenant (saving and transforming of human souls- Deuteronomy 8:18;1 Timothy 2:4;2 Timothy 3:17).

Words of David

"That men may know that thou, whose name alone is Jehovah, art the most high over all the earth."

Psalms 83:18

Words of God Himself

"Behold, I am the Lord, the God of all flesh: is there any thing too hard for me ?" **Jeremiah 32:27**

Words of Paul to the Corinthians

"And God is able to make all grace abound toward you; that ye, always having all sufficiency in all things, may abound to every good work." **2 Corinthians 9:8**

Words of Paul

"For in him we live, and move, and have our being; as certain also of your own poets have said, For we are also his offspring."

Acts 17:28

Your sufficiency is of God

"Not that we are sufficient of ourselves to think any thing as of ourselves; but our sufficiency is of God."

2 Corinthians 3:5

God's daily provisions

"Blessed be the Lord, who daily loadeth us with benefits, even the God of our salvation. Selah."

Psalms 68:19

"It is of the Lord's mercies that we are not consumed, because his compassions fail not. [23] They are new every morning: great is thy faithfulness."

Lamentations 3:22-23

Biblical Financial Truths

Truth #1
Spiritual Blessings

"Blessed be the God and Father of our Lord Jesus Christ, who hath blessed us with all spiritual blessings in heavenly places in Christ."

Ephesians 1:3

Truth #2
God is your source

"Yet thou in thy manifold mercies forsookest them not in the wilderness: the pillar of the cloud departed not from them by day, to lead them in the way; neither the pillar of fire by night, to shew them light, and the way wherein they should go. [20] Thou gavest also thy good spirit to instruct them, and withheldest not thy manna from their mouth, and gavest them water for their thirst. [21] Yea, forty years didst thou sustain them in the wilderness, so that they lacked nothing; their clothes waxed not old, and their feet swelled not."

Nehemiah 9:19-21

You are not your own source (Read Hosea 14:1-3).

Read Jeremiah 17:7-8, for God being your source.

Read Jeremiah 17:5-6, for the results of God not being your source.

INTRODUCTION

"The Lord preserveth all them that love him: but all the wicked will he destroy."

Psalms 145:20

"For of him, and through him, and to him, are all things: to whom be glory for ever. Amen."

Romans 11:36

In Genesis 22:8-14, God is identified as being Jehovah-Jireh (your provider). The word Jehovah means (self existent & self sufficient one). The word Jireh simply means (God will see to it).

God will send you His sustaining Spirit.

"For thou hast been a strength to the poor, a strength to the needy in his distress, a refuge from the storm, a shadow from the heat, when the blast of the terrible ones is as a storm against the wall."

Isaiah 25:4

"Cast thy burden upon the Lord, and he shall sustain thee: he shall never suffer the righteous to be moved."

Psalms 55:22

Additional references. Hebrews 10:19-23; 1 Peter 5:7-8; Psalms 121:1-2; Matthew 6:11 (daily bread); Jeremiah 32:36-41; Nehemiah 5:18; Proverbs 12:3; Psalms 21:7,37:1-13;Isaiah 40:11,25,26;Acts 17:28; 1 Chronicles 29:14; Genesis 48:15 AMP

Truth #3
Pre Ordained Provisions

God has already made provisions through His grace to meet all your financial needs - that your natural needs may be provided for (2 Peter 1:3-4).

"Thou, even thou, art Lord alone; thou hast made heaven, the heaven of heavens, with all their host, the earth, and all things that are therein, the seas, and all that is therein, and thou preservest them all; and the host of heaven worshippeth thee."

Nehemiah 9:6

"O fear the Lord, ye his saints: for there is no want to them that fear him. [10] The young lions do lack, and suffer hunger: but they that seek the Lord shall not want any good thing."

Psalms 34:9-10

"He keepeth the paths of judgment, and preserveth the way of his saints."

Proverbs 2:8

"But my God shall supply all your need according to his riches in glory by Christ Jesus."

Philippians 4:19

The word "all" means meeting every need you have.

Additional references. Psalms 34:9-10; Matthew 6:26-32; 2 Corinthians 9:8; Psalms 84:11; Romans 8:32

Truth #4
Trust only in God

Do not put your trust in man.

In Yourself:

"He that trusteth in his own heart is a fool: but whoso walketh wisely, he shall be delivered."

Proverbs 28:26

You must "Trust in God !" at all times (Psalms 62:8). Remember the great story of Job (Job 1:1-3,14-22, 5:20,13:15,42:10-12). Psalms 33:19, 37:18-19 AMP; Nahum 1:7; Hosea 13:5; Isaiah 40:11; John 10:14.

In Others:

"Thus saith the Lord; Cursed be the man that trusteth in man, and maketh flesh his arm, and whose heart departeth from the Lord. [7] Blessed is the man that trusteth in the Lord, and whose hope the Lord is."

Jeremiah 17:5,7

Additional references. Proverbs 12:5,7; Isaiah 30:1-3; Proverbs 25:19;Psalms 118:8,146:3;Isaiah 2:22,30:18

INTRODUCTION

Do not put your trust in material things or the world's system.

"He that trusteth in his riches shall fall: but the righteous shall flourish as a branch."

Proverbs 11:28

Additional references. Psalms 20:7; Psalms 20:8; Isaiah 36:6; Jeremiah 46:25,48:7; Psalms 16:8

"Woe to them that go down to Egypt for help; and stay on horses, and trust in chariots, because they are many; and in horsemen, because they are very strong; but they look not unto the Holy One of Israel, neither seek the Lord! [2] Yet he also is wise, and will bring evil, and will not call back his words: but will arise against the house of the evildoers, and against the help of them that work iniquity. [3] Now the Egyptians are men, and not God; and their horses flesh, and not spirit. When the Lord shall stretch out his hand, both he that helpeth shall fall, and he that is holpen shall fall down, and they all shall fail together." **Isaiah 31:1-3**

You must learn how to trust only in the one true and living God (2 Samuel 23:5; Nahum 1:7).

"Blessed be the Lord, who daily loadeth us with benefits, even the God of our salvation. Selah."

Psalms 68:19

Additional references. Psalms 5:11, 40:13, 84:12, 121:1-2; Lamentations 3:22-23; Romans 14:23; 1 Timothy 6:17; Trust not in the world (Isaiah 30:2, 31:1,36:6; Jeremiah 2:36; Ezekiel 17:5); James 4:13-16; 2 Chronicles 16:9

In the book of James 1:1-12, you can learn how God wants to teach you how to depend on Him.

Truth #5 *Faithfulness*

God's faithfulness.

"Your faithfulness continues through all generations; you established the earth, and it endures."

Psalms 119:90 NIV

God's faithfulness is unchangeable and perpetual. Psalms 89:2 AMP

"Thy word is true from the beginning: and every one of thy righteous judgments endureth for ever."

Psalms 119:160

"Jesus Christ the same yesterday, and to day, and for ever." **Hebrews 13:8**

See references. Deut. 2:7,7:9; Prov. 10:3; Isaiah 25:1, 43:19; Micah 7:18-20; Luke 1:72-73;Hebrews 6:13-20, 10:23;Joshua 23:14; Acts 4:34-35 (condition of the early church - none suffered lack - all needs were met). See the story in Romans 4:16-21. **God honors His promises (1 Kings 8:56;Psalms 111:9;2 Timothy 2:13).**

INTRODUCTION

Your faithfulness.

"O love the Lord, all ye his saints: for the Lord preserveth the faithful, and plentifully rewardeth the proud doer." **Psalms 31:23**

Additional references.
Job 1:1-3, 42:6,10-13, 5:20,13:15; Philippians 4:4-7; John 15:7; Hebrews 10:35-36, 13:5; James 1:2-5

"In those days there was no king in Israel, but every man did that which was right in his own eyes."

Judges 17:6

When you have no king, you will do what you think is right. You can not truthfully direct your own steps (Proverbs 14:12; Isaiah 53:6; Jeremiah 10:23).

You don't have to sin to have your needs met !

"Saying, When will the new moon be gone, that we may sell corn? and the sabbath, that we may set forth wheat, making the ephah small, and the shekel great, and falsifying the balances by deceit? [6] That we may buy the poor for silver, and the needy for a pair of shoes; yea, and sell the refuse of the wheat? [7] The Lord hath sworn by the excellency of Jacob, Surely I will never forget any of their works."

Amos 8:5-7

INTRODUCTION

Remember to read Romans 12:17.

God will remember how you obtained your money.

One of the reasons why Satan fell is because of dishonest gain.

"Son of man, take up a lamentation upon the king of Tyrus, and say unto him, Thus saith the Lord God; Thou sealest up the sum, full of wisdom, and perfect in beauty. [13] Thou hast been in Eden the garden of God; every precious stone was thy covering, the sardius, topaz, and the diamond, the beryl, the onyx, and the jasper, the sapphire, the emerald, and the carbuncle, and gold: the workmanship of thy tabrets and of thy pipes was prepared in thee in the day that thou wast created. [14] Thou art the anointed cherub that covereth; and I have set thee so: thou wast upon the holy mountain of God; thou hast walked up and down in the midst of the stones of fire. [15] Thou wast perfect in thy ways from the day that thou wast created, till iniquity was found in thee. [16] By the multitude of thy merchandise they have filled the midst of thee with violence, and thou hast sinned: therefore I will cast thee as profane out of the mountain of God: and I will destroy thee, O covering cherub, from the midst of the stones of fire. [17] Thine heart was lifted up because of thy beauty, thou hast corrupted thy wisdom by reason of thy brightness: I will cast thee to the ground, I will lay thee before kings, that they may behold thee. [18] Thou hast defiled thy sanctuaries by the multitude of thine iniquities, by the iniquity of thy traffick; therefore will I bring forth a fire from the midst of thee, it shall devour thee, and I will bring thee to ashes upon the earth in the sight of all them that behold thee."

Ezekiel 28:12-18

CHAPTER 1

WRONG WAYS OF ACQUIRING MONEY

God's principles of honesty must be followed when acquiring money. When something is sinful, even money does not make it right. Read Hebrews 13:18; 1 Timothy 2:2; Acts 24:16; 2 Thessalonians 3:7-9; Proverbs 3:9 AMP, 10:2,12:3,16:8; 1 Timothy 6:5. Dishonest money dwindles away (Proverbs 13:11). Don't mix the unrighteous with the righteous (Deut. 23:18; Proverbs 15:8; 21:27).

Words of Jeremiah on getting riches

"As the partridge sitteth on eggs, and hatcheth them not; so he that getteth riches, and not by right, shall leave them in the midst of his days, and at his end shall be a fool."

Jeremiah 17:11

"Woe unto him that buildeth his house by unrighteousness, and his chambers by wrong; that useth his neighbour's service without wages, and giveth him not for his work."

Jeremiah 22:13

Wrong ways of acquiring money

1. Begging. (You don't have to beg - Proverbs 10:3)

"The steps of a good man are ordered by the Lord: and he delighteth in his way. [24] Though he fall, he shall not be utterly cast down: for the Lord upholdeth him with his hand. [25] I have been young, and now am old; yet have I not seen the righteous forsaken, nor his seed begging bread. [26] He is ever merciful, and lendeth; and his seed is blessed."

Psalms 37:23-26

"Cast not away therefore your confidence, which hath great recompence of reward. [36] For ye have need of patience, that, after ye have done the will of God, ye might receive the promise."

Hebrews 10:35-36

Additional references. Psalms 23:1; Proverbs 20:4; Matthew 17:20; John 15:7,16; 1 John 3:21-22; 1 John 5:13-15; 1 Samuel 2:1,8; Luke 11:5-10,12:32

2. Blood Money.
This is money received from a sinful act that contributes to the destruction of an individual.

Any money that is not acquired honestly is sinful.

"Woe unto him that buildeth his house by unrighteousness, and his chambers by wrong; that useth his neighbor's service without wages, and giveth him not for his work."

Jeremiah 22:13

Leviticus 19:11-13; 2 Kings 5:20-27; Proverbs10:2-3,13:11,15:6,21:6,28:8;Jeremiah 17:11;Amos 8:5-7; Job 27:13,16-17; Romans 12:17; Ephesians 4:28

Even the leaders of Israel would not receive the blood money from Judas Iscariot betrayal of Jesus.

"When the morning was come, all the chief priests and elders of the people took counsel against Jesus to put him to death: [2] And when they had bound him, they led him away, and delivered him to Pontius Pilate the governor. [3] Then Judas, which had betrayeth him, when he saw that he was condemned, repented himself, and brought again the thirty pieces of silver to the chief priests and elders, [4] Saying, I have sinned in that I have betrayed the innocent blood. And they said, What is that to us? see thou to that.

[5] And he cast down the pieces of silver in the temple, and departed, and went and hanged himself. [6] And the chief priests took the silver pieces, and said, It is not lawful for to put them into the treasury, because it is the price of blood." **Matthew 27:1-6**

"Neither repented they of their murders, nor of their sorceries, nor of their fornication, nor of their thefts." **Revelation 9:21**

The word (sorceries) comes from the following Greek words. Pharmakeia, Pharmakeus, Pharmakon, Pharmakos. These words mean medication, drugs, spells, spell-giving potion, poisoning, witchcraft, pharmacist, druggist and magician.

The penalty

1 Corinthians 3:9,16-18, 6:20; Romans 6:13,16,19, 8:1,5-7,13,14, 12:1-2, 13:14; Galatians 5:24,6:8; Jude 1:7-8; 1 Peter 1:14.

Additional scriptures. Malachi 3:5; Romans 14:21; 1 Thessalonians 5:22; Revelation 18:23, 21:8,22:15

Another example of blood money is the selling of spiritual drugs (false religions - doctrines of men) Romans 16:17-18; Galatians 1:8-9, 3:1. The Messiah by the apostate shepherds and sheep. See: Zechariah 11:1-17; Matthew 26:14-16, 27:1-6

3. Selling your body.
Money received from sinful services. This money is not to be used for the worship of God.

"There shall be no whore of the daughters of Israel, nor a sodomite of the sons of Israel. [18] Thou shalt not bring the hire of a whore, or the price of a dog, into the house of the Lord thy God for any vow: for even both these are abomination unto the Lord thy God." **Deuteronomy 23:17-18**

Physical fornication. Jeremiah 3:2; Ezekiel 16:24-25; Micah 1:7; Romans 12:1; 1 Corinthians 6:19; Hebrews 13:4; 2 Cor. 6:16; Revelation 21:8,22:15; Hosea Chapter 2

Spiritual fornication. Doing things the world's way. This includes (harlotry/adultery/incest). Isaiah 57:7-9,23:17;1 Cor. 6:9; Jeremiah 3:2-9;51:7; Nahum 3:4; Hosea 4:12-19;Matt. 5:28; Rev. 2:20-23,17:5,18:1-5

4. Gambling.

This is a spirit of unrighteous covetousness - a strong desire to satisfy a deep hunger of wanting more. This sin is also a spirit of avarice (greed). It leads to poverty (Proverbs 11:24,22:16; Ezekiel 7:19). Even winning will not satisfy you. Income from gambling is considered unjust gain, and this gain will bring trouble to your home (Proverbs 15:27).

"He that loveth silver shall not be satisfied with silver; nor he that loveth abundance with increase: this is also vanity." **Ecclesiastes 5:10**

The answer to your thirst is found in (Psalms 107:9).

Therefore - put off the old man !

"Therefore if any man be in Christ, he is a new creature: old things are passed away; behold, all things are become new."

2 Corinthians 5:17

"Mortify therefore your members which are upon the earth; fornication, uncleanness, inordinate affection, evil concupiscence, and covetousness, which is idolatry."

Colossians 3:5

If not - the result

"For this ye know, that no whoremonger, nor unclean person, nor covetous man, who is an idolater, hath any inheritance in the kingdom of Christ and of God."

Ephesians 5:5

God's final wrath for an idolater

"But the fearful, and unbelieving, and the abominable, and murderers, and whoremongers, and sorcerers, and idolaters, and all liars, shall have their part in the lake which burneth with fire and brimstone: which is the second death."

Revelation 21:8

Don't fall for this temptation.

"But they that will be rich fall into temptation and a snare, and into many foolish and hurtful lusts, which drown men in destruction and perdition."

1 Timothy 6:9

"Wealth [not earned but] won in haste or unjustly or from the production of things for vain or detrimental use [such riches] will dwindle away, but he who gathers little by little will increase [his riches]."

Proverbs 13:11 AMP

In Proverbs 13:11 of the Bible version KJV, the word vanity means (unrighteous labor, not earned, meaningless, unsatisfactory).

"Let your conversation be without covetousness; and be content with such things as ye have: for he hath said, I will never leave thee, nor forsake thee."

Hebrews 13:5

Gambling should be hated and rejected by ALL SAINTS, as Paul indicated. "I have coveted no man's silver, or gold, or apparel." **Acts 20:33**

God hates income generated from the spirit of covetousness (Psalms 10:3 AMP).

As noted in Jeremiah 22:17, income from gambling is dishonest gain.

"For your eyes and your heart are only for your covetousness and dishonest gain, for shedding innocent blood, for oppresion and doing violence."

Jeremiah 22:17 AMP

"But ye are they that forsake the Lord, that forget my holy mountain, that prepare a table for that troop, and that furnish the drink offering unto that number."

Isaiah 65:11

Unbelievers support sin, believers support righteousness (Amos 5:25-27).

You must stop giving God's money to the world (Hosea 2:8-10; Isaiah 39:1-8). You must stop saying: "I don't trust God to meet my needs." (Matthew 6:25-34; Galatians 6:6-8; Philippians 4:11-12,19).

Warning !

- Saints should not keep company with covetous or material lustful people. 1 Corinthians 5:11; James 1:15
- Gambling is not for the saints. Ephesians 5:3
- No inheritance in God's kingdom. Ephesians 5:5
- You must learn how to set your affections on things above. Luke 12:15; Colossians 3:2-6
- You may cause your brother or sister to fall victim to this sinful habit. 1 Corinthians 8:9-13

Gambling is also a spirit of unrighteous lust. A sinful longing for something that is forbidden (Mark 4:19; Romans 1:21,7:7,13:9; James 1:14-15).

Additional references. Exodus 20:17; Proverbs 8:36, 10:2, 12:3,11, 15:27, 27:20, 28:16,20; Ecclesiastes 2:3,8,10,11,8:17; Luke 15:11-30; John 6:12; 1 Corinthians 6:12; Galatians 5:23; Ephesians 3:20, 4:28, 5:3; 2 Thessalonians 3:12; Philippians 4:19; 1 Timothy 5:22; 1 Corinthians 6:9-10; Jeremiah 17:11; James 4:4; 1 John 2:15-16; Galatians 5:16;Psalms 119:36; Ezekiel 22:13,33:31; Isaiah 33:15; 1 Timothy 6:9-10; Hebrews 13:5-6; Exodus 20:3; Habakkuk 2:9-11; Psalms 65:4,10:3 AMP, 73:12. Gambling income brings destruction (Proverbs 10:16; 11:18-19 NIV).

5. Lying. Untruth.

"The getting of treasures by a lying tongue is a vanity tossed to and fro of them that seek death."

Proverbs 21:6

"Lying lips are abomination to the Lord: but they that deal truly are his delight." **Proverbs 12:22**

"Behold, ye trust in lying words, that cannot profit."

Jeremiah 7:8

Examples of dishonest gain from lying are found in 2 Kings 5:20-27 and Acts 5:1-11.

Final destination for liars

"But the fearful, and unbelieving, and the abominable, and murderers, and whoremongers, and sorcerers, and idolaters, and all liars, shall have their part in the lake which burneth with fire and brimstone: which is the second death."

Revelation 21:8

Additional references. Proverbs 6:16-19,12:19,15:6, 20:17; Revelation 22:15

6. Stealing. Taking another person's property.

"Will ye steal, murder, and commit adultery, and swear falsely, and burn incense unto Baal, and walk after other gods whom ye know not; [10] And come and stand before me in this house, which is called by my name, and say, We are delivered to do all these abominations?"

Jeremiah 7:9-10

"Ye shall not steal, neither deal falsely, neither lie one to another. [12] And ye shall not swear by my name falsely, neither shalt thou profane the name of thy God: I am the Lord. [13] Thou shalt not defraud thy neighbour, neither rob him: the wages of him that is hired shall not abide with thee all night until the morning."

Leviticus 19:11-13

"Let him that stole steal no more: but rather let him labour, working with his hands the thing which is good, that he may have to give to him that needeth."

Ephesians 4:28

Additional references. Deuteronomy 24:7; Joshua 6:18-19,7:10-26; Judges 17:2; Hosea 4:2; Proverbs 29:24; Zechariah 5:1-5; Matt. 6:20,15:19-20,19:18; 1 Cor. 6:10; Romans 13:9; 1 Peter 4:15; John 12:6; Acts 5:2-3,7-10; Titus 2:10; Proverbs 10:4,14:23,18:9; Exodus 20:15; Employers (Malachi 3:5; James 5:1-4)

7. Making merchandise of people. False prophets (2 Peter 2:3). Many support others - true and false prophets and neglect their own ministry. This is wrong. 1 Timothy 5:8; Deuteronomy 12:5,10-14; Psalms 132:1-5; Proverbs 28:8; Ezekiel 22:13,27

8. Using unjust scales (Cheating - Proverbs 11:1).

"Divers weights are an abomination unto the Lord; and a false balance is not good." **Proverbs 20:23**

Charging usury (interest) to believers. Exodus 22:25; Leviticus 25:35-37; Deut. 23:19; Ezek. 18:13

Remember the money-changers in Matthew 21:12-13.

Man is to trade with honest scales (weights & measures). Deuteronomy 25:13-16; 1 Thessalonians 4:6

One of the reasons for Inflation is the using of dishonest scales (Amos 8:4-8).

Additional references. Proverbs 20:17; Amos 8:5; Hosea 12:7; Jer. 9:4-6; Zechariah 1:9; Rom. 12:17; Laban's treatment of Jacob (Gen. 29:21-30,31:36-42)

9. Robbing God. This means to defraud God.

To hold back or keep back from God

How ?

"Will a man rob God? Yet ye have robbed me. But ye say, Wherein have we robbed thee? In tithes and offerings. [9] Ye are cursed with a curse: for ye have robbed me, even this whole nation."

Malachi 3:8-9

The story of one man who robbed God - Achan

"But all the silver, and gold, and vessels of brass and iron, are consecrated unto the Lord: they shall come into the treasury of the Lord."

Joshua 6:19

"And Joshua said unto Achan, My son, give, I pray thee, glory to the Lord God of Israel, and make confession unto him; and tell me now what thou hast done; hide it not from me. [20] And Achan answered

Joshua, and said, Indeed I have sinned against the Lord God of Israel, and thus and thus have I done: [21] When I saw among the spoils a goodly Babylonish garment, and two hundred shekels of silver, and a wedge of gold of fifty shekels weight, then I coveted them, and took them; and, behold, they are hid in the earth in the midst of my tent, and the silver under it. [25] And Joshua said, Why hast thou troubled us? the Lord shall trouble thee this day. And all Israel stoned him with stones, and burned them with fire, after they had stoned them with stones. [26] And they raised over him a great heap of stones unto this day. So the Lord turned from the fierceness of his anger. Wherefore the name of that place was called, The valley of Achor, unto this day."

Joshua 7:19-21,25,26

Read the story of Ananias & Sapphira (Acts 5:1-10).

Robbing temples for self gain

"Thou that sayest a man should not commit adultery, dost thou commit adultery? thou that abhorrest idols, dost thou commit sacrilege?"

Romans 2:22

James, the brother of Jesus said money received from robbing God is known as worthless treasure.

WRONG WAYS OF ACQUIRING MONEY

"Go to now, ye rich men, weep and howl for your miseries that shall come upon you. [2] Your riches are corrupted, and your garments are motheaten. [3] Your gold and silver is cankered; and the rust of them shall be a witness against you, and shall eat your flesh as it were fire. Ye have heaped treasure together for the last days."

James 5:1-3

You don't have to sin or serve the devil or any false god in any way, to walk in the true promises of God.

"And go not after other gods to serve them, and to worship them, and provoke me not to anger with the works of your hands; and I will do you no hurt. [7] Yet ye have not hearkened unto me, saith the Lord; that ye might provoke me to anger with the works of your hands to your own hurt."

Jeremiah 25:6-7

Additional references. Psalms 23:1-6, 33:18-21, 37:5,7, 40:1, 121:1-2; Ezekiel 22:29; Amos 3:10

In Psalms 37:16, David wrote - "A little that a righteous man hath is better than the riches of many wicked."

The Word of God teaches you God's provisions for meeting your needs and even giving you the desires of your heart, once you learn how to delight yourself in Him (Philippians 4:14-19 and Psalms 37:3-4).

Just obey and wait on God

"And Jehoshaphat stood in the congregation of Judah and Jerusalem, in the house of the Lord, before the new court, [6] And said, O Lord God of our fathers, art not thou God in heaven? and rulest not thou over all the kingdoms of the heathen? and in thine hand is there not power and might, so that none is able to withstand thee? [7] Art not thou our God, who didst drive out the inhabitants of this land before thy people Israel, and gavest it to the seed of Abraham thy friend for ever? [8] And they dwelt therein, and have built thee a sanctuary therein for thy name, saying, [9] If, when evil cometh upon us, as the sword, judgment, or pestilence, or famine, we stand before this house, and in thy presence, (for thy name is in this house,) and cry unto thee in our affliction, then thou wilt hear and help."

2 Chronicles 20:5-9

Read Hebrews 13:5-6 in the Amplified version for more words of comfort about depending on God to provide for you.

"Thus saith the Lord; Cursed be the man that trusteth in man, and maketh flesh his arm, and whose heart departeth from the Lord."

Jeremiah 17:5

"Cast not away therefore your confidence, which hath great recompence of reward. [36] For ye have need of patience, that, after ye have done the will of God, ye might receive the promise."

Hebrews 10:35-36

Read the book of Haggai chapter 1 - for the results of robbing God of His tithes and offerings.

Additional references. Psalms 34:9-10, 37:19, 55:22, 84:11-12, 89:33; Job 36:11; Proverbs 21:7, 28:20; Ezekiel 33:10-16

10. Bribery. A bribe is money or something of value offered or promised in exchange for a sinful act.

This perverts judgment (1 Samuel 8:1-3) and corrupts the heart (Ecclesiastes 7:7 NIV).

References. Exodus 23:8; 1 Samuel 12:3; Judges 16:4-5; Luke 23:2,14; Esther 3:8-9; Nehemiah 5:14-19; Psalms 26:9-11; Matthew 26:14-16,27:3-9; Amos 2:6,5:12; Isaiah 1:23-24; Acts 8:18; Matthew 4:1-11;28:12-15;Job 15:34-35; Deut. 16:19

11. Oppression. Money received in a deceitful and violating manner. Amos 5:11; Isaiah 49:26; Proverbs 14:31,22:16; Ezek. 18:12-13; Acts 10:38; Jam. 5:1-8 Warning and heritage for oppressors (Job 27:13-23).

CHAPTER 2

MEETING GOD'S COVENANT CONDITIONS

God is the covenant keeping one (Deuteronomy 7:9; Judges 2:1; Nehemiah 1:5; Luke 1:72; Hebrews 13:8). Therefore, you must meet God's covenant conditions to receive God's covenant promises (Psalms 84:11; Exodus 23:22; James 1:25).

"Yea, a man may say, Thou hast faith, and I have works: shew me thy faith without thy works, and I will shew thee my faith by my works." **James 2:18**

"But wilt thou know, O vain man, that faith without works is dead?" **James 2:20**

"For as the body without the spirit is dead, so faith without works is dead also." **James 2:26**

~ Condition #1 ~

Be in God's Family *(2 Cor. 1:20)*

"And if ye be Christ's, then are ye Abraham's seed, and heirs according to the promise." **Galatians 3:29**

How to become a member

Repent (Ephesians 2:8; Romans 10:17; Ezekiel 18:30-32; Mark 2:17; Acts 3:19; 2 Pet. 3:9).

"That if thou shalt confess with thy mouth the Lord Jesus, and shalt believe in thine heart that God hath raised him from the dead, thou shalt be saved. [10] For with the heart man believeth unto righteousness; and with the mouth confession is made unto salvation." **Romans 10:9-10**

Additional references. Genesis 17:1-7; Matthew 6:31-33,7:7-11;Galatians 3:13-14,16;Psalms 23:1-2; Hebrews 7:22,13:5; John 15:7,11; Philippians 4:19; Proverbs 2:8; Water baptism (1 Peter 3:21 AMP)

~ Condition #2 ~

Serve Him

"No man can serve two masters: for either he will hate the one, and love the other; or else he will hold to the one, and despise the other. Ye cannot serve God and mammon." **Matthew 6:24**

Additional references. Deut.10:20,11:13-15,28:14;Job 36:11; Romans 12:6-8;Gal. 6:7;1 Corinthians 12:4-11, 28,15:58; Ephesians 4:11; Phil. 2:4-7; John 12:26; James 1:22; Matthew 4:10,24:45; Mark 10:28-30; Revelation 7:15; Romans 12:3-8,13; 1 Peter 4:10. God meets your needs by serving Him through communicating (providing financial support) to His workers (Philippians 4:15-19).

~ Condition #3 ~

Seek Him First

"Trust in the Lord with all thine heart; and lean not unto thine own understanding. [6] In all thy ways acknowledge him, and he shall direct thy paths."

Proverbs. 3:5-6

First in finances (Proverbs 3:9).

"The Lord is good unto them that wait for him, to the soul that seeketh him." **Lamentations 3:25**

"But seek ye first the kingdom of God, and his righteousness; and all these things shall be added unto you." **Matthew 6:33**

Additional references. John 4:34,5:30; Ephesians 5:17,6:6; Hebrews 10:7,9,11:6; 1 Chronicles 28:9; 2 Chronicles 7:13-14,15:1-4,26:1-5,31:21;**Job 8:5-7**; Psalms 9:9-10, 34:10, 119:2; Ezra 8:22-23; Psalms 107:9; Proverbs 28:5; Isaiah 48:17,55:6

~ Condition #4 ~

Faithful Steward

"He that is faithful in that which is least is faithful also in much: and he that is unjust in the least is unjust also in much. [11] If therefore ye have not been faithful in the unrighteous mammon, who will commit to your trust the true riches? [12] And if ye have not been faithful in that which is another man's, who shall give you that which is your own?"

Luke 16:10-12

Ministry of finance (Nehemiah 9:7-8; Proverbs 3:9; Malachi 3:8,10; Matthew 23:23; Luke 6:38,19:17).

Additional references. Proverbs 28:20; Daniel 6:4; Matthew 24:45;1 Cor. 4:2, 10:18-21; Psalms 31:23; Psalms 101:6; Philippians 4:14-19; Hebrews 3:2,5

~ Condition #5 ~

Support God's Work

Why? (to establish His covenant - Deut. 8:18)

• To bring life. It is the responsibility of the saints to support the work of God that the lost may be saved.

"The labour of the righteous tendeth to life: the fruit of the wicked to sin." **Proverbs 10:16**

Prov. 24:11-12;Phil. 2:16; Rom. 12:3-8,13;1 Pet. 4:10; Eph. 4:28-30.

• To bring life more abundantly. John 10:10

God's grace is given according to your giving

"But this I say, He which soweth sparingly shall reap also sparingly; and he which soweth bountifully shall reap also bountifully. [7] Every man according as he purposeth in his heart, so let him give; not grudgingly, or of necessity: for God loveth a cheerful giver. [8] And God is able to make all grace abound toward you; that ye, always having all sufficiency in all things, may abound to every good work."

2 Corinthians 9:6-8

"Insomuch that we desired Titus, that as he had begun, so he would also finish in you the same grace also. [7] Therefore, as ye abound in every thing, in faith, and utterance, and knowledge, and in all diligence, and in your love to us, see that ye abound in this grace also." **2 Corinthians 8:6-7**

"Now unto him that is able to do exceeding abundantly above all that we ask or think, according to the power that worketh in us." **Ephesians 3:20**

- To please God. Philippians 4:18 AMP
- To deliver souls from the devil. Psalms 49:15,82:3-5; Romans 1:16 AMP
- To have God meet your needs. Philippians 4:14-19
- Keep people out of hell. Rev. 21:7-8;Rom. 10:9-17
- To be blessed of God. Psalms 35:27-28, 41:1-3
- To be rich in good works. 1 Tim. 6:18; Phil. 4:15-17

- To obey God's law. 1 Corinthians 9:8; 1 John 5:3; Malachi 3:8-9;Matt. 5:17-18,42,23:23; Luke 11:42; Eph. 2:10,4:28,6:6; Col. 1:10; Prov. 3:9;Heb. 7:5,8
- To bless God. Matthew 25:31-46
- Sealed fruit. Matt. 6:19-21; Phil. 4:17;Rom. 15:25-28
- To help saints grow to fullness in the statue and character of God. Eph. 4:11-13;Col. 1:28;Rom. 15:29
- To avoid lack. Proverbs 28:27; Malachi 3:11; Luke 6:38; Acts 4:32,34,20:28; Jeremiah 3:15,23:4
- To avoid God's judgement. Matthew 10:11-15
- To help stay the hands of leaders. Exodus 17:9-13
- To not lose the kingdom of God. Matthew 21:33-44

God will remember your support (Jeremiah 17:10; Hebrews 6:10; Luke 14:13-14; Ephesians 6:8).

Additional references. Job 36:11; 2 Corinthians 8:15, 9:7-8,9:9-10 (No sowing - No harvest); Genesis 8:22,26:12; Isaiah 55:10; Galatians 6:9; Malachi 3:10-11; Luke 6:38; Philippians 4:14-19; Matthew 6:19-21; Psalms 126:6;Proverbs 11:25,30,31,19:17; Matthew 19:29; Romans 4:16; Jer. 31:16. The primary ways of support are with tithes and offerings.

~ Condition #6 ~
Right Motives

"Ye ask, and receive not, because ye ask amiss, that ye may consume it upon your lusts." **James 4:3**

Once you have met your covenant conditions, or have done the will of God, God will surely honor His part of the covenant and manifest His promises.

"He sent redemption unto his people: he hath commanded his covenant for ever: holy and reverend is his name." **Psalms 111:9**

"And I will make an everlasting covenant with them, that I will not turn away from them, to do them good; but I will put my fear in their hearts, that they shall not depart from me." **Jeremiah 32:40**

"For ye have need of patience, that, after ye have done the will of God, ye might receive the promise." **Hebrews 10:36**

"But let patience have her perfect work, that ye may be perfect and entire, wanting nothing." **James 1:4**

Promises of the godly in this life

"Praise ye the Lord. Blessed is the man that feareth the Lord, that delighteth greatly in his commandments. [2] His seed shall be mighty upon earth: the generation of the upright shall be blessed. [3] Wealth and riches shall be in his house: and his righteousness endureth for ever." **Psalms 112:1-3**

Additional references. Romans 8:27; 1 John 5:13-14

~ Condition #7 ~
Fear God

"The secret of the LORD is with them that fear him; and he will shew them his covenant."

Psalms 25:14

"O fear (reverence) the Lord, ye his saints: for there is no want to them that fear (reverence) him."

Psalms 34:9

Additional references. Psalms 111:5,112:1-3, 145:19; Proverbs 15:16,22:4; Ecclesiastes 8:12; Isaiah 33:6; Luke 1:50; Psalms 15:4,31:19,33:18-19,62:5-8;119:38; John 15:5

~ Condition #8 ~
Patience

The word patience means to endure testing (the trial of your faith - 1 Peter 1:7,4:12) with a victorious attitude (Romans 4:21,23 5:3-5).

The character of patience will allow you to:

- Keep the commandments of God. Revelation 14:12
- Destroy the spirit of lack. James 1:4
- Inherit your land. Psalms 37:34
- Manifest the promises of God. Job 14:14, 42:10; Hebrew 6:12,10:36; Matthew 21:22; Rom. 4:16-21; Rom. 6:13-15
- Cause your needs to be fulfilled. Psalms 104:27

CHAPTER 3

GOD'S WAYS OF MEETING YOUR FINANCIAL NEED$

God is your true source. The following covenant channels (ways) have been ordained by God as His resources to meet (satisfy) all your financial needs.

Words of encouragement

From Jesus

"Teaching them to observe all things whatsoever I have commanded you: and, lo, I am with you alway, even unto the end of the world. Amen."

Matthew 28:20

From Paul

"Therefore, my beloved brethren, be ye stedfast, unmovable, always abounding in the work of the Lord, forasmuch as ye know that your labour is not in vain in the Lord."

1 Corinthians 15:58

Identify your calling (work). Isaiah 54:16;John 2:5, 4:34;Romans 11:29;Deuteronomy 31:6;Joshua 1:5; Hebrews 13:5. You must always abide in your right divine calling. 1 Corinthians 7:20; 1 Kings 2:3, 8:56.

Way #1

Your Job (talents/gifts/skills - Proverbs 3:5-6)

Most people today, even the saints of God are only familiar with this way. You must learn to stop limiting God (2 Chronicles 16:9 Part A; Psalms 78:40-41).

"And the Lord God took the man, and put him into the garden of Eden to dress it and to keep it."

Genesis 2:15

Additional references. Genesis 3:23; Deut. 30:8-10; Prov. 10:4,12:11,14,13:11,13:4,19:15,16:3,26,28:19; Exodus 20:9,36:1-4, 34:21; 2 Chronicles 1:11-12, 15:7,24:20,26:5; Jer. 25:6-7; 1 Thessalonians 4:11-12; 2 Thessalonians 3:10; Ecclesiastes 9:10,10:18; 2 Peter 1:10; 1 Peter 2:18 (learn to be submissive); Galatians 6:5; James 1:25; Daniel 6:4 (be faithful).

Do not overwork yourself (Mark 2:27,6:30-31,8:36).

Earn your income with righteous labor

"Honor the Lord with your capital and sufficiency [from righteous labors] and with the firstfruits of all your income." **Proverbs 3:9 AMP**

See also. Ezekiel 22:12-13 and Proverbs 21:25

Work with the right attitude

Your motivation for work - should be that of working for the Lord

"And whatsoever ye do, do it heartily, as to the Lord, and not unto men; [24] Knowing that of the Lord ye shall receive the reward of the inheritance: for ye serve the Lord Christ." **Colossians 3:23-24**

Genesis 31:4-7; Matthew 6:24,20:26; Luke 6:31; Prov. 23:4; Jer. 17:5,7;Gal. 6:4 AMP;Eph. 6:5-8;1 Tim. 6:9;2 John 1:8; Rev. 22:7,12

Work with the right behavior

"And that ye study to be quiet, and to do your own business, and to work with your own hands, as we commanded you; [12] That ye may walk honestly toward them that are without, and that ye may have lack of nothing." **1 Thessalonians 4:11-12**

You must prove faithful (Luke 16:10-12; 1 Cor. 4:2).

When you look at it as your ministry, you will realize that you are working for God (Ephesians 2:10,6:8; 1 Corinthians 15:58). This becomes full time ministry (known as work-place ministry). Let your light shine. Remember, your promotion will come from God (Proverbs 22:29; Psalms 75:6-7; Ecclesiastes 5:12; 1 Sam. 2:6; 2 Chronicles 15:7; Ruth 2:12; 1 Peter 5:6).

God must anoint your gift that it may prosper you and others - as He did for others (Exodus 31:1-6,35:31,35,38:23; Deut. 34:9; Acts 1:13-15,2:1-4).

Additional References. Exodus 28:3, 40:13-15 (all priests - Exodus 19:6, 1 Peter 2:9); Ephesians 5:18; 1 John 2:27; Joshua 1:7-8;1 Samuel 2:7-8;Rev. 22:12

Way #2 Your Business

- Find your true market place ministry. Prov. 3:5-6; Matt. 7:7-8,27:57; Acts 16:14,18:1-3; Luke 16:19-31
- Commit your work (business) to God. Prov. 16:3 AMP
- Plan your work. Prov. 21:5; Matt. 6:24,7:12; Phil. 2:4
- Avoid laziness. Prov. 10:4; Matt. 25-26; Rom. 12:11
- Stay focus & faithful. Prov. 23:4,28:19-22; Is. 30:21; Joshua 1:7-8; Jeremiah 22:13; Gal. 6:9; Matt. 27:57
- Follow Godly counsel. 2 Chron. 24:20; Prov. 3:5-6, 12:15,15:22,19:20-21; 2 Sam. 22:31-33;Isaiah 48:17
- Honor God with your time. Rom. 14:5; Heb. 10:25
- Honor God with your $$. Prov. 3:9-10; Luke 19:1-10; Malachi 3:8-10; Matt. 23:23; 1 Cor. 16:2; Heb. 7:5,8
- Honor your employees. Lev. 19:13; Deut. 24:14-15; Hosea 12:7; Zech. 7:9-10; Malachi 3:5; James 5:1-8

See other references. Prov. 15:22, 22:29, 23:4-5, 24:30-31; John 6:27;Isaiah 46:10;Psalms 18:30,32; 2 Samuel 22:31,33; 1 Kings 9:26-28, 10:11,12; Mark 6:3,4:4; 2 Chron. 8:17-18,9:21,26:3-5; Prov. 11:1, 13:11,16:11 AMP, 31:10-31; 1 Thess. 4:11; Acts 16:14,18:3; Psalms 1:3; Luke 14:28; James 5:1-6; 1 Timothy 6:9-10; 2 Corinthians 6:14; John 21:1-6

Way #3

Ministry Office (Acts 22:10; 2 Timothy 1:9)

"Wherefore the rather, brethren, give diligence to make your calling and election sure: for if ye do these things, ye shall never fall." **2 Peter 1:10**

Find your true 5-fold ministry calling (Eph. 4:11-13;Prov. 16:3)

See also. Deuteronomy 17:9-11;Malachi 2:7; Acts 6:4

"Even so hath the Lord ordained that they which preach the gospel should live of the gospel."
1 Corinthians 9:14

"Let him that is taught in the word communicate unto him that teacheth in all good things." **Galatians 6:6**

See: 1 Chronicles 28:20-21; 2 Chronicles 31:4; Matthew 28:20; 1 Corinthians 7:20,9:7-11,15:58; 2 Corinthians 9:8;Rom. 8:28,15:25-27; Heb. 7:1-11

Examples of God's sustaining spirit

(Psalms 37:1-13; Luke 11:9-13, 12:31; Hebrews 10:19-23; 1 Peter 5:7-8)

- Joseph's daily needs met. Genesis 48:15, 39:2
- Joseph's family & nations. Genesis 42:25, 41:56-57
- Nation of Israel for forty years. Nehemiah 9:21
- King Solomon. 1 Kings 4:7
- The ministry of Elijah. 1 Kings 17:1-6,9-16
- The work of Nehemiah. Nehemiah 5:14-19
- The ministry of Jesus. Luke 8:1-3; Mark 6:3
- The ministry of Paul. Philippians 4:14-19; Acts 18:1-3, 20:34-35; 2 Corinthians 11:9; 1 Thessalonians 2:9

In 1 Kings 17:4, the word "command" means to appoint, charge, or set in order.

All five-fold ministry ministers (Ephesians 4:11-12) must really learn how to depend on God (Luke 22:35 AMP; 2 Timothy 1:12). Other ministry workers (1 Corinthians 9:13). Be very careful to avoid this temptation (2 Kings Chapter 5). Read 1 Timothy 5:17-18.

God will sustain you, even in the times of famine. Job 5:20;Psalms 37:18-19, 33:19; Isaiah 25:4 AMP; 1Peter 4:19

Way #4

Your Natural Family

"A good man leaveth an inheritance to his children's children: and the wealth of the sinner is laid up for the just." **Proverbs 13:22**

"But if any provide not for his own, and specially for those of his own house, he hath denied the faith, and is worse than an infidel." **1 Timothy 5:8**

"But if any widow have children or nephews, let them learn first to shew piety at home, and to requite their parents: for that is good and acceptable before God." **1 Timothy 5:4**

"Behold, the third time I am ready to come to you; and I will not be burdensome to you: for I seek not yours, but you: for the children ought not to lay up for the parents, but the parents for the children." **2 Corinthians 12:14**

Additional references. Genesis 25:5,31:10-16,48:15; Deuteronomy 6:7,10-12; 1 Chronicles 28:7-8,29:19; Job 42:15; Psalms 78:1-4, 112:2; Proverbs 13:24,19:14,31:15-31; Isaiah 38:19; Ephesians 6:4; Numbers 27:8-11; Isaiah 58:7; Hebrews 11:20-21

Way #5

Your Spiritual Family

(All believers/members in the family of God)

"Then they that gladly received his word were baptized: and the same day there were added unto them about three thousand souls. [42] And they continued stedfastly in the apostles' doctrine and fellowship, and in breaking of bread, and in prayers. [43] And fear came upon every soul: and many wonders and signs were done by the apostles. [44] And all that believed were together, and had all things common; [45] And sold their possessions and goods, and parted them to all men, as every man had need."

Acts 2:41-45

Faithfulness of the early church

"And when they had prayed, the place was shaken where they were assembled together; and they were all filled with the Holy Ghost, and they spake the word of God with boldness. [32] And the multitude of them that believed were of one heart and of one soul: neither said any of them that ought of the things which he possessed was his own; but they had all things common. [33] And with great power gave the apostles witness of the resurrection of the Lord Jesus: and great grace was upon them all. [34] Neither was there any among them that lacked: for as many as were possessors of lands or houses sold them, and brought the prices of the things that were sold, [35] And laid them down at the apostles' feet: and distribution was made unto every man according as he had need."

Acts 4:31-35

"Then the disciples, every man according to his ability, determined to send relief unto the brethren which dwelt in Judaea."

Acts 11:29

Remember to do good to your brothers & sisters

"As we have therefore opportunity, let us do good unto all men, especially unto them who are of the household of faith." **Galatians 6:10**

Additional references. Exodus 23:9-11; Deuteronomy 15:7-11; Proverbs 3:27-28; Galatians 2:10; 1 John 3:17,4:20,2:4; Eph. 2:19,4:28; Romans 12:13,15:25-26; 1 Corinthians 16:1-2; 2 Corinthians 8:1-5,14,9:12,11:9; 2 Samuel 9:6-7; 1 Timothy 3:2; Philippians 4:10-19; Hebrews 10:33-34,13:1-3; James 2:14-16; 2 Thess. 3:6-10; Joshua 22:6-8

Way #6

Uncommon or Unexplained Blessings

"For my thoughts are not your thoughts, neither are your ways my ways, saith the Lord."

Isaiah 55:8

"Behold, ye despisers, and wonder, and perish: for I work a work in your days, a work which ye shall in no wise believe, though a man declare it unto you."

Acts 13:41

The source of good gifts

"Every good gift and every perfect gift is from above, and cometh down from the Father of lights, with whom is no variableness, neither shadow of turning."

James 1:17

The widow woman of Zarephath

"Arise, get thee to Zarephath, which belongeth to Zidon, and dwell there: behold, I have commanded a widow woman there to sustain thee. [10] So he arose and went to Zarephath. And when he came to the gate of the city, behold, the widow woman was there gathering of sticks: and he called to her, and said, Fetch me, I pray thee, a little water in a vessel, that I may drink. [11] And as she was going to fetch it, he called to her, and said, Bring me, I pray thee, a morsel of bread in thine hand. [12] And she said, As the Lord thy God liveth, I have not a cake, but an handful of meal in a barrel, and a little oil in a cruse: and, behold, I am gathering two sticks, that I may go in and dress it for me and my son, that we may eat it, and die. [13] And Elijah said unto her, Fear not; go and do as thou hast said: but make me thereof a little cake first, and bring it unto me, and after make for thee and for thy son. [14] For thus saith the Lord God of Israel, The barrel of meal shall not waste, neither shall the cruse of oil fail, until the day that the Lord sendeth rain upon the earth. [15] And she went and did according to the saying of Elijah: and she, and he, and her house, did eat many days. [16] And the barrel of meal wasted not, neither did the cruse of oil fail, according to the word of the Lord, which he spake by Elijah." **1 Kings 17:9-16**

The children of Israel. Exodus 11:2-3, 16:11-15,35, 12:35; Joshua 5:12. The widow's oil (2 Kings 4:1-7).

Additional references. Job 42:10-15; Isaiah 43:19,58:9;Psalms 78:23-25;Ecclesiastes 9:11,11:5; Matthew 14:18-21; Ephesians 3:20. Money being placed into the mouth of a fish (Matthew 17:27).

In Proverbs 8:12, the word prudence means discretion and witty (practical wisdom - good timing).

When God reveals a witty idea to you, His wisdom will direct you in bringing the Idea into manifestation (Isaiah 48:17; Jacob - Genesis 31:11-13, 30:29-43).

Way #7

Transfer of Wealth (Inheritance of the Heathen)

A covenant with God - Psalms 111:5-6

Why God desires to bless you financially !

- To enhance your life (Proverbs 8:21,24:4; 3 John 2)
- To leave an inheritance to your children (Proverbs 13:22)
- To establish His covenant (the saving & transforming of human souls (Deut. 8:18; 1 Timothy 2:4; 2 Timothy 3:17)
- To Help the needy (1 Timothy 6:17-19)
- To express God's love (1 John 3:17)
- To work and receive a sure reward (Proverbs 10:16,11:18)

A heathen person is a gentile or non-believer in God.

"This is the portion of a wicked man with God, and the heritage of oppressors, which they shall receive of the Almighty. [16] Though he heap up silver as the dust, and prepare raiment as the clay; [17] He may prepare it, but the just shall put it on, and the innocent shall divide the silver. [18] He buildeth his house as a moth, and as a booth that the keeper maketh. [19] The rich man shall lie down, but he shall not be gathered: he openeth his eyes, and he is not." **Job 27:13,16-19**

"Ask of me, and I shall give thee the heathen for thine inheritance, and the uttermost parts of the earth for thy possession." **Psalms 2:8**

"A good man leaveth an inheritance to his children's children: and the wealth of the sinner is laid up for the just." **Proverbs 13:22**

"For God giveth to a man that is good in his sight wisdom, and knowledge, and joy: but to the sinner he giveth travail, to gather and to heap up, that he may give to him that is good before God. This also is vanity and vexation of spirit." **Ecclesiastes 2:26**

Past wealth transfer

(Joseph - Genesis 45:8,13, 47:13-26);
(Joseph's family - Genesis 47:11);
(Israel -Exodus 12:34-36;Joshua Chapters 13 -19);
(David - 2 Samuel 8:10-12);
(The four lepers - 2 Kings 7:1-8);
(Judah - 2 Chronicles 20:1-25)

Additional wealth transfer references

Galatians 3:17,18,29; Genesis 13:15, 17:7-8;
Ezekiel 7:19,11:17; Matthew 5:5,13:12, 25:14-30;
Job 27:13-17; James 5:1-8; Isaiah 23:18,60:1-6,61:6;
Daniel 7:18,22,27;Zech. 8:1-16,14:1,14;Haggai 2:7;
Micah 4:13;Psalms 2:8,37:9,29,49:10; Prov. 28:8;
Joel 2:21-27; Romans 8:17; Rev. 11:15,21:24-27

Never give up on God. The Lord is always able to make His grace abound in your life (2 Corinthians 9:8). In essence, the Lord will make a way some how (Genesis 22:14; Psalms 37:5; Daniel 3:17,26).

Remember - God is able !

Prayer of Jeremiah

"Ah Lord God! behold, thou hast made the heaven and the earth by thy great power and stretched out arm, and there is nothing too hard for thee."

Jeremiah 32:17

God's response

"Behold, I am the Lord, the God of all flesh: is there any thing too hard for me?" **Jeremiah 32:27**

God is your very present help, in the time of need (Psalms 46:1,5,91:15; Isaiah 65:24; Jeremiah 33:3; Luke 1:37).

New Testament miracles

God supernaturally put money in the mouth of a fish for the paying of taxes

"Notwithstanding, lest we should offend them, go thou to the sea, and cast an hook, and take up the fish that first cometh up; and when thou hast opened his mouth, thou shalt find a piece of money: that take, and give unto them for me and thee."

Matthew 17:27

God multiplied food

"But Jesus said unto them, They need not depart; give ye them to eat. [17] And they say unto him, We have here but five loaves, and two fishes. [18] He said, Bring them hither to me. [19] And he commanded the multitude to sit down on the grass, and took the five loaves, and the two fishes, and looking up to heaven, he blessed, and brake, and gave the loaves to his disciples, and the disciples to the multitude. [20] And they did all eat, and were filled: and they took up of the fragments that remained twelve baskets full. [21] And they that had eaten were about five thousand men, beside women and children." **Matthew 14:16-21**

David knew the real source of his help

"Cast thy burden upon the Lord, and he shall sustain thee: he shall never suffer the righteous to be moved." **Psalms 55:22**

David says in Psalms 23:1 (AMP), "THE LORD is my Shepherd [to feed, guide, and shield me], I shall not lack."

Additional references. Psalms 91:1-12; 1 Peter 5:7; Psalms 145:14-16; 2 Kings 4:1-7 (widow woman)

Way #8 Investment Income

This type of income is money gained from participating in an activity where money is placed at risk - except for the kingdom of God (Genesis 8:21-22) - for the purpose of making an honest financial profit.

A foolish man spends all he earns (Proverbs 21:20).

The Investment Process !

- God supplies the seed (money). 2 Corinthians 9:10; Hosea 2:8; John 3:27. Only - if you are a sower !!!
- You prepare the soil/ground. Isaiah 28:24-26 AMP; Deut. 14:5; Jer. 4:1-3; Hosea 10:12; Prov. 28:19
- You sow (invest/plant) the seed. Luke 19:12-24; Luke 6:38; 2 Corinthians 9:6; Gal. 6:7; Heb. 4:2; Leviticus 27:30; Malachi 3:10-11;John 12:24

  Sow in good soil. Isaiah 32:20 AMP; Matt. 13:23; Eccl. 11:1
- You water (nurture) the seed. Ecclesiastes 11:4,6; Proverbs 18:20-21; Malachi 3:13-14; 1 Corinthians 3:5-8; Galatians 6:9; Hebrews 4:2; Proverbs 12:14

  Thank God for the increase. Deut. 26:10-15; Psalms 147:7-8
- Protect the seed. Lev. 26:15-16; Deut. 28:15,33,38, 51; Prov. 18:21; Mal. 3:13-14;Micah 6:15; Jer. 12:13
- God multiplies (increases) the seed. Gen. 8:22; Gen. 26:12; Lev. 26:3-5;2 Chron. 26:1,5;Ps. 126:5-6; Deut. 11:14; Hos. 2:8; 1 Cor. 3:6;2 Cor. 9:10;Jer. 5:24
- Honor God. Lev. 27:30;Deut. 26:2;Prov. 3:9 AMP; Mal. 3:10; Matt. 23:23; 1 Cor. 16:2; 2 Cor. 9:8-13

Let's look at receiving investment income from the following six (6) biblical investment considerations.

1) Why should I invest ?

- To obey the command of God. Matthew 25:27; Luke 19:11-26 (Parable of the pounds)
- To provide for family needs. 1 Timothy 5:8
- To be able to give more. Luke 12:48,19:12-26
- To promote the saving gospel. Proverbs 10:16; Romans 10:9-17; Philippians 4:16; Rev. 21:7-8
- To promote the transforming gospel. 1 Tim. 1:4; Romans 12:2;2 Timothy 3:16-17;Ephesians 4:11-15
- To overcome future calamities. Genesis 41:29-35
- To leave an inheritance. Proverbs 13:22, 19:14, 21:20, 30:24-25; Ecclesiastes 7:11; 2 Cor. 12:14
- To set an example for others. Matthew 25:14-30

2) When should I invest ?

- Now. Don't wait for all conditions to be favorable. There will always be an element of risk outside the kingdom of God. See reference Ecclesiastes 11:4. You can't control the risk. However, you can minimize it by doing your home work (Proverbs 24:27). If you fail, try again (Psalms 37:23-24;Prov. 24:16).

3) Where should I invest ?

- The kingdom of God. This represents God's true Christian ministries. There is always opportunity to invest and receive a sure return. Genesis 8:22; Zechariah 8:12; Matt. 9:37-38; 2 Corinthians 8:4. The greatest investment you can ever make is into the kingdom of God. Mal. 3:10-12 (unlimited return);Prov. 8:19 AMP,11:30,19:17;Matt. 6:19-21, 33,19:29; Luke 6:38; Psalms 126:6; Galatians 6:9.

Why You Should Invest Into The Kingdom of God

(A) There is no greater investment than honoring God by contributing to the salvation and the transformation of souls. This type of investment is known as a spiritual investment. **(B)** This investment yields eternal rewards (Philippians 4:17; 1 Peter 1:3-4; Revelation 22:12; Matthew 6:20; 1 Timothy 6:19). **(C)** It also yields earthly rewards (Proverbs 11:31; Luke 6:38). All non-spiritual investments are only temporal or temporary (2 Corinthians 4:18).

- Other places of financial investments. Savings; Gold; Mutual Funds; Stocks; Real Estate; Your business; Other business owners; Life Insurance; IRAs; College Planning; Charitable Gift Annuity; US Treasury Bonds; US Treasury TIPS; and Witty (practical) Godly ideas (Proverbs 8:12).

See the story of the parable of talents - Matt. 25:14-30.

4) How should I invest ?

- Make God your senior partner. Proverbs 3:5-6
- Seek Godly counsel. Psalms 32:8,33:11,37:23; 119:24;Prov. 12:15;Lev. 19:31;Isaiah 9:6;Heb. 4:12; Prov. 11:14,15:22,19:20-21;2 Samuel 22:31,33; Job 37:16; Deut. 29:9; Eccl. 12:13; Isaiah 46:10, 48:17; Joshua 1:8; Proverbs 28:25
- Be led by the Spirit. John 16:13; 1 Cor. 2:9-11
- Avoid unwise investments. Ecclesiastes 5:13-14; Prov. 13:11,24:27,29:24 (avoid the thief);Rev. 3:18
- Diversify wisely. Eccl. 11:2; Lev. 19:19; Deut. 22:9

5) How much should I invest ?

- Not everything. Luke 12:16-21,34
- Establish a budget. Luke 14:28-30; John 6:1-12
- General rule. Between 5 &10% (outside the kingdom)

6) How long should I wait ?

Learn to be patient and consistent

(consistently invest, even if only a little at a time)

"Dishonest money dwindles away, but he who gathers money little by little makes it grow."

Proverbs 13:11 NIV

In Proverbs 19:2 (AMP), King Solomon said: When you disregard knowledge, get in a hurry, this will cause you to sin and miss the mark. See Prov. 21:5

Wait until your season comes due (Leviticus 26:4; Deuteronomy 11:14;Ezekiel 34:26-27;Hebrews 6:7).

"And let us not be weary in well doing: for in due season we shall reap, if we faint not." **Galatians 6:9**

Learn to be patient, prayerful and praiseful

"Be careful for nothing; but in every thing by prayer and supplication with thanksgiving let your requests be made known unto God." **Philippians 4:6**

Remember to seek Christian professionals - such as financial advisors, investors, trust and estate planning attorneys, accountants, tax consultants and other industry related professionals. See references Psalms 1:1, Psalms 37:30-31 and Proverbs 15:22.

CHAPTER 4

THE DESIRES OF YOUR HEART

God will give you the desires of your heart, when you learn how to truthfully delight yourself in Him.

The word "desires" means (requests or petitions). Hebrew - Mish'alah - "Mish-aw-law". Strong #4862.

"Therefore I say unto you, What things soever ye desire, when ye pray, believe that ye receive them, and ye shall have them." **Mark 11:24**

"The sacrifice of the wicked is an abomination to the Lord: ***but the prayer of the upright is his delight***." **Proverbs 15:8**

"For the Lord God is a sun and shield: the Lord will give grace and glory: no good thing will he withhold from them that walk uprightly." **Psalms 84:11**

"Delight thyself also in the Lord; and he shall give thee the desires of thine heart. [5] Commit thy way unto the Lord; trust also in him; and he shall bring it to pass." **Psalms 37:4-5**

THE DESIRES OF YOUR HEART

The word delight means soft or pliable. To humble yourself - which leads to your wealthy place in God.

"Thou openest thine hand, and satisfiest the desire of every living thing. [19] He will fulfil the desire of them that fear him: he also will hear their cry, and will save them." **Psalms 145:16,19 See Psalms 10:17**

David knew this

"Praise ye the Lord. Blessed is the man that feareth the Lord, that delighteth greatly in his commandments. [2] His seed shall be mighty upon earth: the generation of the upright shall be blessed. [3] Wealth and riches shall be in his house: and his righteousness endureth for ever." **Psalms 112:1-3**

Ways of delighting yourself in God

- First be reconciled to God. Job 22:21-26; Psalms 149:4
- Obedience. 1 Sam. 15:22; Psalms 40:8; 1 John 3:22
- Seeking Godly counsel. Psalms 1:1-3
- Seeking God. Isaiah 56:4, 58:2; Psalms 16:11
- Meditating on God's word. Psalms 1:2 AMP, 112:1,119:16, 24,35,77,143,174; Rom. 7:22;1 Pet. 2:2-3;2 Tim 3:15-17
- Praying. Psalms 145:18; Prov. 15:8; Mark 11:24;Rev. 8:3-4
- Praying for others. 1 Timothy 2:1-3
- Receiving God's goodness. Nehemiah 9:24-25
- Resting in the spiritual sabbath. Isaiah 58:13-14; Col. 2:16
- Resting in the comforts of God. Psalms 94:19
- Rejoicing in God. Prov. 8:30; Psalms 28:7; Job 8:21
- Understand and know God. Jer. 9:24; Rom. 1:28
- Support God's work. Phil. 4:18 AMP, Heb. 13:16;2 Cor. 9:7
- Practicing a true fast. Isaiah 58:13-14

THE NEED MEETER

- Practice lovingkindness, justice & righteousness. Jer. 9:24
- Love the Wisdom of God. Proverbs 8:11, 29:3
- Exercise faith. Hebrews 11:6
- Uprightness of heart. 1 Chronicles 29:17
- Be blameless. Proverbs 11:20
- Praise. Psalms 95:1-2; Hebrews 13:15-16
- Praiseful singing. Psalms 69:30-31
- Worship. Psalms 95:6-7; John 4:23, 9:31; Rev. 4:11
- Deal faithfully and truthfully. Prov. 11:20,12:22 (NIV)
- Fear God. Psalms 145:19, 147:11 (AMP); Acts 10:35
- Walk after the Spirit (by faith) not after the flesh. Rom. 8:4,8

Hanna petitioned God for a male child -
He gave her the prophet Samuel

"So Hannah rose up after they had eaten in Shiloh, and after they had drunk. Now Eli the priest sat upon a seat by a post of the temple of the Lord. [10] And she was in bitterness of soul, and prayed unto the Lord, and wept sore. [11] And she vowed a vow, and said, O Lord of hosts, if thou wilt indeed look on the affliction of thine handmaid, and remember me, and not forget thine handmaid, but wilt give unto thine handmaid a man child, then I will give him unto the Lord all the days of his life, and there shall no razor come upon his head. [17] Then Eli answered and said, Go in peace: and the God of Israel grant thee thy petition that thou hast asked of him. [20] Wherefore it came to pass, when the time was come about after Hannah had conceived, that she bare a son, and called his name Samuel, saying, Because I have asked him of the Lord. [27] For this child I prayed; and the Lord hath given me my petition which I asked of him."

1 Samuel 1:9-11,17,20,27

Hezekiah petitioned God to extend his life - God extended his life with 15 more years and healed his body from sickness

"In those days was Hezekiah sick unto death. And Isaiah the prophet the son of Amoz came unto him, and said unto him, Thus saith the Lord, Set thine house in order: for thou shalt die, and not live. [2] Then Hezekiah turned his face toward the wall, and prayed unto the Lord, [3] And said, Remember now, O Lord, I beseech thee, how I have walked before thee in truth and with a perfect heart, and have done that which is good in thy sight. And Hezekiah wept sore. [4] Then came the word of the Lord to Isaiah, saying, [5] Go, and say to Hezekiah, Thus saith the Lord, the God of David thy father, I have heard thy prayer, I have seen thy tears: behold, I will add unto thy days fifteen years. [6] And I will deliver thee and this city out of the hand of the king of Assyria: and I will defend this city. [7] And this shall be a sign unto thee from the Lord, that the Lord will do this thing that he hath spoken; [8] Behold, I will bring again the shadow of the degrees, which is gone down in the sun dial of Ahaz, ten degrees backward. So the sun returned ten degrees, by which degrees it was gone down. [9] The writing of Hezekiah king of Judah, when he had been sick, and was recovered of his sickness."

Isaiah 38:1-9

Your desires are good in God's eyes

"The desire of the righteous is only good: but the expectation of the wicked is wrath."

Proverbs 11:23

God wants you to live in His promises because it glorifies Him

"If ye abide in me, and my words abide in you, ye shall ask what ye will, and it shall be done unto you. [8] Herein is my Father glorified, that ye bear much fruit; so shall ye be my disciples."

John 15:7-8

"For verily I say unto you, That whosoever shall say unto this mountain, Be thou removed, and be thou cast into the sea; and shall not doubt in his heart, but shall believe that those things which he saith shall come to pass; he shall have whatsoever he saith."

Mark 11:23

"For all the promises of God in him are yea, and in him Amen, unto the glory of God by us."

2 Corinthians 1:20

Remember Solomon's request

The key is to ask - Matthew 7:7-11

"And Solomon said, Thou hast shewed unto thy servant David my father great mercy, according as he walked before thee in truth, and in righteousness, and in uprightness of heart with thee; and thou hast kept for him this great kindness, that thou hast given him a son to sit on his throne, as it is this day. [7] And now, O Lord my God, thou hast made thy servant king instead of David my father: and I am but a little child: I know not how to go out or come in. [8] And thy servant is in the midst of thy people which thou hast chosen, a great people, that cannot be numbered nor counted for multitude. [9] Give therefore thy servant an understanding heart to judge thy people, that I may discern between good and bad: for who is able to judge this thy so great a people?"

1 Kings 3:6-9

God's response

"And the speech pleased the Lord, that Solomon had asked this thing. [11] And God said unto him, Because thou hast asked this thing, and hast not asked for thyself long life; neither hast asked riches for thyself, nor hast asked the life of thine enemies; but hast asked for thyself understanding to discern judgment; [12] Behold, I have done according to thy words: lo, I have given thee a wise and an understanding heart; so that there was none like thee before thee, neither after thee shall any arise like unto thee. [13] And I have also given thee that which thou hast not asked, both riches, and honour: so that there shall not be any among the kings like unto thee all thy days. [14] And if thou wilt walk in my ways, to keep my statutes and my commandments, as thy father David did walk, then I will lengthen thy days."

1 Kings 3:10-14

God vowed to bless Solomon with all that his soul desired (1 Kings 11:37-38).

Read the prayer of Jabez in 1 Chronicles 4:10.

The apostle John's confidence of prayer

"And this is the confidence that we have in him, that, if we ask any thing according to his will, he heareth us: [15] And if we know that he hear us, whatsoever we ask, we know that we have the petitions that we desired of him."

1 John 5:14-15

The future desires of all nations will be transferred into the kingdom of God

"And I will shake all nations and the desire and the precious things of all nations shall come in, and I will fill this house with splendor, says the Lord of hosts."

Haggai 2:7 AMP

Jesus' expression of His true love for the faithful

"If ye abide in me, and my words abide in you, ye shall ask what ye will, and it shall be done unto you. [11] These things have I spoken unto you, that my joy might remain in you, and that your joy might be full."

John 15:7,11

Acknowledgements of God's faithfulness

"For all the promises of God in him are yea, and in him Amen, unto the glory of God by us."

2 Corinthians 1:20

"Let us hold fast the profession of our faith without wavering; (for he is faithful that promised)."

Hebrews 10:23

"If they obey and serve him, they shall spend their days in prosperity, and their years in pleasures."

Job 36:11

Additional references. Psalms 10:17,35:27,36:8,84:11; Proverbs 10:24; James 4:2, 5:16; 1 Thessalonians 5:17; 1 John 3:21-22; Isaiah 1:19; 1 Timothy 6:17; Matthew 6:33,7:11,21:22; Romans 2:11; Luke 12:32

You must always trust God, to meet your every need (Psalms 37:40; Hebrews 10:23). God will not only meet your needs, the more you please Him, you will abound in His grace (2 Cor. 9:8;1 Thess. 4:1). **A-men´**

Other Books by Dr. Robert Mukes

What To Do With Money™

Would you like to learn God's principles for managing money faithfully ? In this book, Dr. Mukes teaches you the real truth about money. Are you prepared to give a true account of your stewardship ? This book teaches you how to get prepared. (152 Pages)

To order:

on the web at: www.amazon.com

I Know I'm Saved™

This book is a practical guide to understanding what true salvation really is. (85 Pages)

To order:

on the web at: www.amazon.com

Made in United States
Troutdale, OR
11/03/2026

56844448R00042